The United States "Easy" Wars and Diplomatic Maneuvering

Copyright Page

TITLE: The United States "Easy" Wars and Diplomatic Maneuvering

1ST Edition

Table of Contents

The United States "Easy" Wars and Diplomatic Maneuvering

By Roberto Miguel Rodriguez

Chapter 1: The United States "Easy" Wars: Panama, Grenada, and Kuwait

The Invasion of Panama

In the annals of American military interventions, the Invasion of Panama stands as a pivotal moment that forever altered the geopolitical landscape of Latin America and the Caribbean. This subchapter delves deep into the details of this controversial operation, shedding light on the United States' hidden agendas and diplomatic maneuvering.

The year was 1989, and tensions were brewing between the United States and Panama's authoritarian leader, General Manuel Noriega. The United States had long been concerned about Noriega's alleged involvement in drug trafficking and his increasingly hostile stance towards American interests in the region. Fueled by these concerns, the United States orchestrated a full-scale invasion of Panama, codenamed Operation Just Cause.

Under the guise of restoring democracy and protecting American lives, the United States military swiftly deployed over 26,000 troops to Panama, overwhelming the Panamanian defense forces. The invasion was met with both support and criticism, with some hailing it as a necessary action to remove a dictator, while others condemned it as a blatant act of aggression.

This subchapter examines the hidden agendas behind the invasion, revealing the United States' ulterior motives beyond the stated goal of restoring democracy. It explores the strategic importance of the Panama Canal Zone and the American military presence in the region, highlighting how the invasion further consolidated American dominance.

Moreover, it delves into the United States' military interventions during the Cold War era, casting the invasion of Panama as part of a broader pattern of American military actions in response to perceived threats to its interests. It also explores the links between the Invasion of Panama and other "easy" wars, such as the interventions in Grenada and Kuwait.

For diplomats seeking a comprehensive understanding of United States military interventions in Latin America, the Caribbean, and other strategic regions, this subchapter offers valuable insights. It sheds light on the complex dynamics between the United States and smaller nations, as well as the role of diplomacy in justifying military actions.

Ultimately, the Invasion of Panama serves as a cautionary tale, reminding diplomats of the need for transparency, respect for sovereignty, and a careful consideration of the long-term consequences of military interventions. By examining this pivotal moment in history, diplomats can gain a deeper understanding of the United States' "easy" wars and the diplomatic maneuvering that accompanied them.

Background and Justification for Intervention

The United States has a long history of military interventions, particularly in regions that are of strategic importance or where American interests are at stake. This subchapter aims to provide diplomats with an in-depth understanding of the background and justification for such interventions, focusing on the United States "Easy" Wars: Panama, Grenada, and Kuwait.

One of the key factors behind American military interventions in these countries is the protection of American citizens and interests. The United States has consistently viewed its role as the global protector of democracy and human rights, and has intervened in cases where these principles are threatened. In Panama, for example, the United States intervened to remove Manuel Noriega, a dictator accused of drug trafficking and human rights abuses. Similarly, in Grenada, the intervention was justified based on the need to protect American medical students and prevent the establishment of a communist regime.

In addition to protecting its citizens, the United States has also intervened in these regions to safeguard its economic interests. The Gulf region, for instance, is a major supplier of oil to the global market, and any disruption in the flow of oil would have dire consequences for the American economy. Therefore, military operations in the Gulf region, such as the intervention in Kuwait, were driven by the need to ensure a stable oil supply and protect American economic interests.

Furthermore, the United States has frequently used military interventions as a means of maintaining its dominance and influence in the world. During the Cold War, for instance, American military interventions were often aimed at countering the spread of communism and preventing the expansion of Soviet influence. This was evident in Central America, where the United States intervened in countries like Nicaragua and El Salvador to support anti-communist forces and prevent the establishment of pro-Soviet governments.

It is important to note, however, that American military interventions have not always been met with universal support. Critics argue that such interventions can be driven by hidden agendas, including economic interests, geopolitical dominance, and the desire to secure resources. These critics often point to instances where American interventions have resulted in unintended consequences, such as civilian casualties, political instability, and resentment towards the United States.

In conclusion, the background and justification for American military interventions in the United States "Easy" Wars: Panama, Grenada, and Kuwait, as well as other regions, are complex and multifaceted. While the protection of American citizens and interests, promotion of democracy and human rights, and safeguarding economic stability have often been cited as reasons for intervention, there is also a need to critically examine the underlying motivations and potential consequences of such actions. Diplomats must engage in a thorough analysis of these factors in order to make informed decisions and pursue policies that align with the principles of international cooperation and peacekeeping.

Operation Just Cause: Planning and Execution

In the annals of American military history, Operation Just Cause stands as a testament to the meticulous planning and flawless execution of a military intervention. This subchapter delves into the intricacies of this operation, providing diplomats with valuable insights into the United States' "easy" war in Panama.

Planning for Operation Just Cause commenced long before the actual execution, with the United States closely monitoring the actions of Panamanian leader Manuel Noriega. Noriega's oppressive regime and his involvement in drug trafficking had become a growing concern for American interests in the region. As a result, the United States began crafting a comprehensive plan to remove Noriega from power and restore stability in Panama.

The operation itself was a testament to the efficiency and precision of the United States military. Extensive intelligence gathering, involving both human assets and advanced surveillance technology, allowed American forces to gain a comprehensive understanding of the terrain, key targets, and potential threats. This information formed the basis for a meticulously crafted plan that aimed to neutralize Noriega's forces swiftly and minimize civilian casualties.

The execution of Operation Just Cause was a textbook example of military precision. American forces launched a surprise attack, swiftly seizing control of vital infrastructure such as the Panama Canal and key military installations. The operation involved a combination of special forces, air support, and ground troops, all working in perfect harmony to achieve their objectives. The operation's success can be attributed to the careful coordination between different branches of the military and the seamless integration of intelligence, logistics, and combat capabilities.

Operation Just Cause also exemplified the United States' commitment to minimizing collateral damage and protecting civilian lives. Extensive measures were taken to ensure the safety of innocent Panamanians caught in the crossfire. The operation was conducted with surgical precision, aiming to neutralize Noriega's forces while minimizing civilian casualties and damage to critical infrastructure.

This subchapter serves as a valuable resource for diplomats interested in understanding the planning and execution of Operation Just Cause. By analyzing this case study, diplomats can gain insights into the United States' approach to military interventions in small-scale conflicts, American military actions in response to perceived threats to American interests, and U.S. military interventions in oil-rich countries. It also sheds light on the United States' military involvement in Central America, American military operations in the Gulf region, and American military engagements in small island nations.

Overall, Operation Just Cause serves as a testament to the United States' ability to plan and execute military interventions with precision and efficiency. By studying this operation, diplomats can gain valuable lessons that can inform their own strategic approaches in future conflicts.

Consequences and Legacy of the Invasion

The 1989 invasion of Panama by the United States had far-reaching consequences and left a lasting legacy in various aspects, ranging from diplomatic relations to military interventions. This subchapter aims to delve into the significant consequences of the invasion and its subsequent legacy, shedding light on its impact on the United States' "Easy" Wars and Diplomatic Maneuvering.

First and foremost, the invasion of Panama had a profound effect on the United States' military interventions in Latin America. It set a precedent for future interventions, establishing a sense of confidence and assertiveness in the region. The success of the Panama invasion bolstered the notion that the United States could swiftly and effectively intervene in small-scale conflicts to protect its interests.

Furthermore, the invasion shaped the United States' military actions in the Caribbean. It demonstrated that the United States was willing to use force to maintain stability and protect its strategic assets in the region. This had implications for American military operations in the Gulf region as well, as it emboldened the US to take decisive action to safeguard its interests in oil-rich countries.

In terms of diplomatic relationships, the invasion strained the United States' ties with several nations. It was seen by many as an infringement on Panama's sovereignty and a violation of international law. Diplomats from various countries expressed concern over the unilateral approach of the United States and its disregard for international norms.

The legacy of the invasion also extended to the Panama Canal Zone and American military presence in the region. It spurred discussions about the necessity of maintaining a significant military presence in Panama, leading to a reassessment of American military bases worldwide.

Moreover, the invasion had repercussions for U.S. military involvement in Central America. It heightened fears of potential interventions, causing countries in the region to be cautious and wary of the United States' intentions. This legacy continued throughout the Cold War era, as American military interventions were often perceived as preemptive measures to protect American interests.

In conclusion, the consequences and legacy of the invasion of Panama were far-reaching and had a significant impact on various aspects of United States' military interventions and diplomatic maneuvering. It set a precedent for future interventions, strained diplomatic relationships, and shaped the perception of American military actions in the region. The invasion left a lasting legacy that continues to influence American military engagements in small-scale conflicts, oil-rich countries, and perceived threats to American interests. Diplomats and individuals interested in these niches will find valuable insights into the consequences and long-term impact of the invasion.

The Invasion of Grenada

In the annals of United States military interventions, the invasion of Grenada in 1983 stands out as a prime example of a seemingly "easy" war. However, beneath the surface, hidden agendas and intricate diplomatic maneuvering played a crucial role in shaping this controversial chapter in American history.

Grenada, a tiny Caribbean island nation with a population of just over 100,000, was thrust into the international spotlight when a Marxist coup took place in 1979. The newly established People's Revolutionary Government (PRG) under Prime Minister Maurice Bishop aligned itself with communist powers like Cuba, raising concerns in Washington about the spread of Soviet influence in the region. As the Cold War tensions escalated, the United States viewed Grenada as a potential threat to its interests in the Caribbean.

In 1983, the fragile political situation in Grenada reached a breaking point when internal power struggles within the PRG led to Bishop's house arrest and subsequent execution. Fearing a power vacuum and potential Soviet expansion, the United States swiftly responded with Operation Urgent Fury, a military invasion of Grenada.

While the official rationale for the invasion was to protect American citizens and restore democracy, hidden agendas were at play. The United States sought to send a clear message to its enemies that it would not tolerate Soviet encroachment in its backyard. Additionally, the invasion served as a demonstration of American military might and resolve, intended to deter other countries in the region from aligning with communist forces.

Internationally, the invasion of Grenada sparked widespread condemnation from countries critical of American unilateralism. Diplomats from around the world expressed concerns about the violation of national sovereignty and the disregard for the United Nations Charter. The United States defended its actions by citing the Treaty of Mutual Assistance and Cooperation, a regional agreement between several Caribbean nations, including Grenada, which allowed for collective security measures.

In retrospect, the invasion of Grenada highlighted the complexities and contradictions of American military interventions during the Cold War era. It underscored the United States' willingness to act unilaterally when it perceived threats to its interests, often bypassing diplomatic channels and international consensus. The Grenada invasion also marked a turning point in Latin America and the Caribbean, as it fueled anti-American sentiment and reinforced the notion of American imperialism in the region.

For diplomats and those interested in the United States' "easy" wars, the invasion of Grenada remains a case study in the interplay between military actions, diplomatic maneuvering, and hidden agendas. It serves as a cautionary tale, reminding us of the need for careful evaluation and consideration of the long-term consequences of military interventions, particularly in small island nations and oil-rich countries.

Context and Rationale for U.S. Intervention

Introduction:

In this subchapter, we will delve into the context and rationale behind the United States' interventions in various regions and conflicts. By understanding the historical backdrop and the underlying reasons for these interventions, diplomats can gain valuable insights into U.S. foreign policy and its impact on the world stage.

Historical Context:

The United States' interventionist approach can be traced back to the Cold War era, where the country sought to contain the spread of communism. This era witnessed American military engagement in Latin America, the Caribbean, and the Gulf region, among others. The Panama Canal Zone and American military presence in strategic locations played a pivotal role in safeguarding American interests.

Rationale for Intervention:

1. Protection of American Interests:

One of the primary motivations for U.S. intervention was the protection of American interests, particularly in oil-rich countries. America's dependence on oil necessitated the safeguarding of crucial resources to ensure economic stability and national security.

2. Response to Perceived Threats:

American military actions were often prompted by perceived threats to national security or American interests. Small-scale conflicts or regional tensions were seen as potential threats that could escalate and harm U.S. allies or the world order. Hence, swift intervention was deemed necessary.

3. Humanitarian Concerns:

U.S. military involvement in Central America and other regions was driven by humanitarian concerns, aiming to protect civilian populations from oppressive regimes or violent conflicts. The United States sought to promote democracy, stability, and human rights in these nations.

4. Defense of Democratic Values:

The United States, as a democratic nation, felt compelled to defend democratic values and institutions wherever they were threatened. This ideology played a crucial role in interventions in places like Grenada, where American citizens were at risk or democratic regimes were under threat.

Conclusion:

Understanding the context and rationale behind U.S. interventions allows diplomats to analyze the underlying factors that shape American foreign policy. The protection of American interests, response to perceived threats, humanitarian concerns, and defense of democratic values have been consistent factors driving U.S. military engagements. By comprehending these dynamics, diplomats can navigate the intricacies of U.S. foreign policy and foster meaningful dialogue and cooperation between nations.

Operation Urgent Fury: Objectives and Tactics

In the chapter titled "Operation Urgent Fury: Objectives and Tactics" from the book "Hidden Agendas: The United States' 'Easy' Wars and Diplomatic Maneuvering," we delve into one of the most significant military interventions of the United States in the Caribbean. This subchapter aims to provide diplomats, especially those interested in the United States' military interventions, with a comprehensive understanding of the objectives and tactics employed during Operation Urgent Fury.

Operation Urgent Fury was launched in October 1983, as a response to the deteriorating political situation in Grenada. The primary objective of this military intervention was to restore democratic governance and protect American citizens on the island. Additionally, the United States sought to prevent the establishment of a Soviet-backed government that could potentially threaten American interests in the region.

To achieve these objectives, the United States employed a combination of conventional and unconventional tactics. One of the key elements of the operation was the rapid deployment of a joint task force, consisting of the U.S. Army, Navy, Air Force, and Marines. This allowed for swift and decisive action on multiple fronts, ensuring the success of the mission.

The tactics employed during Operation Urgent Fury included a combination of amphibious assaults, airborne operations, and helicopter insertions. These tactics were specifically designed to neutralize the enemy forces while minimizing civilian casualties and infrastructure damage. The use of precision airstrikes, coupled with ground operations, played a crucial role in achieving the desired objectives.

Furthermore, the United States prioritized gathering intelligence to identify the locations of enemy forces, key infrastructure, and potential threats to American interests. This intelligence-driven approach allowed for effective targeting and minimized the risk to American forces.

In addition to the military tactics, diplomatic maneuvering was also an integral part of Operation Urgent Fury. The United States worked closely with regional partners, such as the Organization of Eastern Caribbean States, to garner support for the intervention. This collaboration helped legitimize the operation and ensured a unified approach among the countries involved.

Operation Urgent Fury serves as a prime example of the United States' military engagement in small-scale conflicts and its commitment to protecting American interests in the Caribbean. The objectives and tactics employed during this operation highlight the intricate balance between military force and diplomacy.

Overall, this subchapter provides diplomats and individuals interested in the United States' military interventions with a comprehensive overview of the objectives and tactics employed during Operation Urgent Fury. By understanding the intricacies of this operation, diplomats can gain valuable insights into the complexities of military engagements and their impact on diplomatic relations in the region.

Aftermath of the Invasion and Regional Impact

The aftermath of any military invasion is often filled with complex challenges and unintended consequences. The United States' "Easy" Wars of Panama, Grenada, and Kuwait were no exception. These military interventions had a far-reaching regional impact, particularly in Latin America, the Caribbean, Central America, and the Gulf region. As diplomats, it is crucial to understand the consequences of these military actions and their implications for American interests and global diplomacy.

In Latin America, the United States' military interventions had mixed results. While the invasion of Panama in 1989 successfully removed the authoritarian regime of Manuel Noriega, it also sparked widespread resentment and anti-American sentiments in the region. The United States' military involvement in Latin America during the Cold War, particularly in countries like Nicaragua and El Salvador, further strained diplomatic relations and fueled political instability.

In the Caribbean, the United States' military actions had varying degrees of success. The invasion of Grenada in 1983 was seen as a swift and decisive victory, restoring stability and democracy. However, it also raised concerns about American imperialism and the violation of sovereignty. The American military presence in the Panama Canal Zone was another contentious issue, with Panama eventually regaining control of the canal in 1999.

Central America witnessed significant repercussions from American military involvement. The United States' interventions in countries like Guatemala, Honduras, and Nicaragua during the Cold War had long-lasting effects, including civil wars, displacement of populations, and economic instability. These interventions were often driven by perceived threats to American interests, such as communism and drug trafficking.

The Gulf region also experienced the aftermath of American military operations. The liberation of Kuwait in 1991 was hailed as a successful example of international cooperation, but it also raised questions about American motives and long-term involvement in the region. Subsequent military engagements in Iraq and Afghanistan further complicated the regional dynamics and strained diplomatic relations.

In small island nations and oil-rich countries, American military interventions had significant economic and political implications. The United States' interventions in countries like Haiti and the Dominican Republic aimed to restore stability, but they also highlighted the challenges of nation-building and the complexities of interventionist policies. In oil-rich countries like Iraq and Libya, American military actions had far-reaching consequences for global energy markets and regional stability.

Overall, the aftermath of the United States' "Easy" Wars and military interventions had a profound regional impact. As diplomats, it is essential to critically examine these actions, understanding their successes and failures, and finding diplomatic solutions to mitigate the unintended consequences. The book "Hidden Agendas: The United States' 'Easy' Wars and Diplomatic Maneuvering" provides valuable insights into these issues, guiding diplomats in their efforts to navigate the complex aftermath of military interventions and promote peace, stability, and cooperation in the affected regions.

The Gulf War: Liberation of Kuwait

The Gulf War, also known as Operation Desert Storm, marked a significant turning point in the history of American military interventions in the Gulf region. The liberation of Kuwait from Iraqi aggression showcased the United States' commitment to protecting its interests and maintaining stability in the oil-rich countries of the Middle East.

In the 1980s, Iraq, under the leadership of Saddam Hussein, had emerged as a regional power in the Gulf. The Iran-Iraq War had left Iraq heavily indebted, and Saddam viewed Kuwait as an easy target to resolve his financial woes. In August 1990, Iraqi forces invaded Kuwait, swiftly occupying the country and threatening the stability of the entire region.

The United States, recognizing the importance of Kuwait as a strategic partner and a major oil supplier, swiftly responded to the crisis. President George H.W. Bush rallied international support and formed a coalition of nations, including the United Kingdom, France, and Saudi Arabia, to counter Iraq's aggression. This multinational force, authorized by the United Nations, was determined to liberate Kuwait and restore stability in the region.

The military operation that followed was meticulously planned and executed. American air power played a crucial role in the initial phase of the conflict, launching a massive aerial bombardment on Iraqi targets. This barrage severely weakened Iraq's defenses and paved the way for a ground invasion.

In February 1991, a coalition ground offensive was launched, spearheaded by American forces. The highly coordinated operation swiftly pushed Iraqi troops out of Kuwait, liberating the country within a matter of days. The United States' military superiority was on full display during this campaign, with advanced weaponry and superior training giving them a decisive advantage.

The Gulf War demonstrated the United States' unwavering commitment to protecting its interests and maintaining stability in the Gulf region. It also highlighted the effectiveness of international cooperation when faced with a common threat. The liberation of Kuwait not only restored the sovereignty of a small nation but also sent a clear message to other potential aggressors in the region.

However, the Gulf War also raised important questions about the long-term consequences of American military interventions in oil-rich countries. Critics argued that the United States' involvement was driven by its desire to protect its access to Gulf oil reserves, rather than purely humanitarian concerns. This criticism fueled debates about the United States' hidden agendas and its role as the world's policeman.

In conclusion, the Gulf War stands as a significant chapter in the United States' military engagements in the Gulf region. The liberation of Kuwait showcased American military might and underscored its commitment to protecting its interests in oil-rich countries. However, it also sparked debates about the motives behind American interventions and the potential consequences of such actions. As diplomats, it is crucial to analyze these events critically and understand the complexities of the United States' "easy" wars and diplomatic maneuvering in the Gulf region and beyond.

Causes and Justification for Intervention

In the realm of international relations, the decision to intervene in the affairs of other nations is a complex and multifaceted issue. The United States, as one of the world's leading superpowers, has frequently found itself engaged in military interventions throughout history. This subchapter aims to shed light on the causes and justification behind such interventions, focusing on the United States' "easy" wars and diplomatic maneuvering.

When assessing the causes for intervention, diplomats must consider the geopolitical interests of the United States. The American government often intervenes when its strategic, economic, or security interests are threatened. This has been particularly evident in regions such as Latin America, the Caribbean, and the Gulf, where the United States has historically maintained significant influence.

In many cases, American military interventions have been prompted by perceived threats to American interests. These threats can range from political instability and human rights abuses to economic disruptions and the control of vital resources. For example, the United States' military actions in oil-rich countries have often been driven by the need to secure access to crucial energy supplies and protect American economic interests.

Furthermore, the United States has frequently justified its interventions as responses to small-scale conflicts or perceived threats. In the context of the Cold War, American military interventions were often framed as necessary to contain the spread of communism and prevent the rise of Soviet influence. This rationale was particularly evident in interventions in Central America, where the United States sought to counter left-wing movements seen as aligned with the Soviet Union.

Another key factor influencing American interventions has been the presence of military bases and installations. The Panama Canal Zone, for instance, played a significant role in shaping American military presence and interventions in the region. These bases serve as strategic assets, allowing the United States to project power and protect its interests more effectively.

In conclusion, the causes and justifications for American military interventions are diverse, with a range of factors influencing the decision-making process. Diplomats must carefully consider geopolitical interests, perceived threats to American interests, the control of vital resources, and the presence of military installations. Understanding these complexities is essential for comprehending the United States' "easy" wars and diplomatic maneuvering, as well as the broader context of American military interventions in various regions and conflicts.

Operation Desert Storm: Coalition Building and Strategy

In the subchapter titled "Operation Desert Storm: Coalition Building and Strategy" from the book "Hidden Agendas: The United States' 'Easy' Wars and Diplomatic Maneuvering," we delve into the intricate web of coalition building and strategic planning that led to the successful military intervention during the Gulf War.

Addressed primarily to diplomats and audiences interested in various niches such as United States military interventions in Latin America, American military actions in the Caribbean, U.S. military involvement in Central America, and many more, this subchapter sheds light on the behind-the-scenes negotiations, alliances, and intricacies that paved the way for the coalition's success.

Operation Desert Storm marked a turning point in modern warfare. The United States, along with a diverse coalition of international partners, executed a swift and decisive military campaign to liberate Kuwait from Iraqi forces. However, the victory was not achieved through military might alone. It was the result of careful diplomatic maneuvering and strategic planning.

The subchapter begins by examining the process of coalition building. Diplomats played a crucial role in persuading nations across the globe to join forces against Saddam Hussein's aggression. The United States leveraged its diplomatic relationships, emphasizing the importance of protecting international law and preserving global security. Through skillful negotiation and diplomacy, a broad coalition was formed, uniting nations with diverse interests and backgrounds.

Furthermore, the subchapter delves into the intricacies of the military strategy employed during Operation Desert Storm. The United States, backed by its coalition partners, meticulously planned the air campaign, ground offensive, and naval operations. The objective was not only to liberate Kuwait but also to minimize civilian casualties and collateral damage.

The subchapter also highlights the importance of intelligence sharing and coordination between the coalition partners. It explores how diplomats and military leaders worked together to gather accurate and actionable intelligence, enabling precise targeting and minimizing risks to both military personnel and innocent civilians.

Ultimately, Operation Desert Storm showcased the effectiveness of international cooperation in achieving military objectives while minimizing the potential for protracted conflicts. It demonstrated that diplomatic negotiations and strategic planning can be as vital to success as military might.

For diplomats and those interested in the United States' military interventions in various regions, this subchapter provides valuable insights into the complexity of coalition building, strategic planning, and diplomatic maneuvering. It serves as a reminder that military engagements should always be approached with careful consideration of diplomatic efforts, international partnerships, and the preservation of global security.

Implications and Long-Term Effects of the Conflict

As diplomats and professionals engaged in international affairs, it is essential for us to understand the implications and long-term effects of conflicts, particularly those involving the United States. In this subchapter, we will delve into the consequences of the "Easy" Wars and the United States' diplomatic maneuvering during and after these conflicts.

The United States' military interventions in Latin America, the Caribbean, Central America, and the Gulf region have left lasting impressions on both the targeted nations and the global stage. These actions were often motivated by perceived threats to American interests, such as the protection of democracy, safeguarding vital resources, or countering communism during the Cold War era.

One of the notable implications of these conflicts is the erosion of trust and strained diplomatic relations between the United States and the affected countries. The perception of American imperialism or interventionism has created resentment and deep-seated animosity, which continues to influence diplomatic negotiations and regional dynamics to this day. It is crucial for diplomats to acknowledge and address these historical wounds to build stronger, more cooperative relationships.

Furthermore, the long-term effects of these conflicts have had a profound impact on the targeted nations' socio-political landscapes. In some cases, these interventions have resulted in political instability, economic devastation, and the erosion of democratic institutions. It is imperative for diplomats to recognize and support the development of sustainable governance structures, economic recovery, and social cohesion in these countries, as they are essential for long-term stability and the promotion of mutual interests.

Moreover, American military interventions in oil-rich countries have had significant ramifications for global energy security and regional stability. The United States' involvement in conflicts such as Kuwait and other Gulf nations has highlighted the delicate balance between securing vital resources and respecting national sovereignty. Diplomats must navigate these complexities, promoting dialogue and cooperation to ensure that energy resources are managed transparently and equitably.

Lastly, the "Easy" Wars and other small-scale conflicts have underscored the importance of multilateralism and international cooperation. Diplomats must actively engage with regional organizations, such as the United Nations or the Organization of American States, to foster collaborative approaches to conflict prevention, resolution, and post-conflict reconstruction.

In conclusion, the implications and long-term effects of the United States' "Easy" Wars and diplomatic maneuvering have had far-reaching consequences for both the targeted nations and the global community. As diplomats, it is our responsibility to acknowledge these historical legacies, address grievances, and promote sustainable peace, stability, and prosperity through effective diplomacy and international cooperation.

Chapter 2: United States Military Interventions in Latin America

American Military Actions in the Caribbean

The United States' military actions in the Caribbean have been a subject of significant debate and scrutiny, especially among diplomats and those interested in the United States' "easy" wars and diplomatic maneuvering. This subchapter explores the historical context, motivations, and consequences of American military interventions in the Caribbean region.

Throughout the 20th century, the United States exerted its military power in the Caribbean for various reasons, predominantly driven by its strategic interests and perceived threats to American security. The United States' military interventions in the Caribbean were often motivated by concerns over political instability, economic interests, and the protection of American citizens and properties.

One notable example is the United States' military involvement in Central America during the Cold War era. In an effort to counter the spread of communism, the United States intervened militarily in countries such as Guatemala, Nicaragua, and El Salvador. These interventions were often characterized by covert operations, support for local anti-communist forces, and even direct military interventions.

Another significant aspect of American military actions in the Caribbean was its involvement in small island nations. The United States, with its dominant naval power, often asserted its influence in these nations to protect American interests, particularly in relation to trade routes and access to resources. The Panama Canal Zone and American military presence in Panama is a prime example of this, where the United States ensured its control over the strategic canal for decades.

Moreover, American military interventions in the Caribbean were also influenced by the region's oil-rich countries. The United States sought to protect its access to oil reserves, especially during times of political instability or threats to American interests. This led to military actions in countries like Venezuela and the Dominican Republic, where the United States aimed to safeguard its energy security.

It is important to note that American military interventions in the Caribbean were not without controversy. Critics argue that these actions often undermined local sovereignty, perpetuated political instability, and resulted in unintended consequences such as civil unrest and anti-American sentiments.

In conclusion, American military actions in the Caribbean have shaped the region's history and continue to be topics of interest for diplomats and those studying United States' military interventions. These actions were driven by various factors, including strategic interests, perceived threats, and the protection of American economic and political interests. While some argue that these interventions were necessary for American security, others criticize them for their impacts on local sovereignty and stability. Understanding the complexities and consequences of these military actions is essential for diplomats and policymakers dealing with the region.

Historical Context and Motivations for Intervention

In the subchapter "Historical Context and Motivations for Intervention," we delve into the underlying factors that have historically influenced the United States' decision to intervene militarily in various regions around the world. This analysis aims to provide diplomats with a comprehensive understanding of the historical context and motivations that have shaped American military interventions.

The United States has been involved in several "easy" wars, such as Panama, Grenada, and Kuwait. These interventions were often driven by a combination of factors, including protecting American citizens and interests, ensuring regional stability, and upholding democratic values. For instance, the Panama intervention in 1989 was motivated by the need to safeguard the Panama Canal and protect American lives and property in the region.

Similarly, American military interventions in Latin America during the Cold War were heavily influenced by the perceived threat of communism. The United States believed that by intervening in countries like Cuba and Nicaragua, it could prevent the spread of Soviet influence and protect its own national security interests. These interventions often had long-lasting repercussions, shaping the political landscape of the region for many years to come.

In the Caribbean, American military actions were driven by concerns over political instability and the protection of American economic interests. The United States sought to maintain stability in the region, particularly in countries like Haiti and the Dominican Republic, to ensure the smooth flow of trade and protect American investments.

The Panama Canal Zone and American military presence were closely tied to the strategic importance of the canal for American trade and defense. The United States maintained a military presence in the region to safeguard its control over the canal and ensure its uninterrupted operation.

In the Gulf region, American military operations were often motivated by the need to protect access to oil resources and maintain stability in this crucial area. The interventions in countries like Iraq and Kuwait were driven by the desire to safeguard American economic interests and ensure the global flow of oil.

Furthermore, the United States has frequently intervened in small island nations and oil-rich countries due to perceived threats to American interests. These interventions aimed to protect American allies, counter potential threats, and secure vital resources.

In conclusion, understanding the historical context and motivations behind American military interventions is essential for diplomats to navigate the complexities of international relations. By comprehending these factors, diplomats can effectively engage with the United States on matters related to its military engagements, small-scale conflicts, and response to perceived threats to American interests.

Cases of Intervention: Dominican Republic and Haiti

The subchapter "Cases of Intervention: Dominican Republic and Haiti" delves into two significant instances of United States military involvement in the Caribbean region. This chapter aims to provide diplomats and individuals interested in the various facets of American military interventions with a comprehensive understanding of these specific cases and their implications.

The Dominican Republic and Haiti, neighboring countries in the Caribbean, have experienced political instability, economic struggles, and social unrest throughout their histories. The United States, driven by its interests and concerns for stability in the region, intervened in both nations to protect its interests and ensure favorable outcomes.

In the case of the Dominican Republic, the United States' intervention in 1965 came in response to a violent political crisis and the growing influence of communism in the country. The chapter explores the motivations behind the intervention, highlighting the United States' desire to prevent the spread of communism and protect American investments in the region. It also delves into the diplomatic maneuvering employed by the United States to justify its military presence and the subsequent consequences of its intervention.

Similarly, the chapter explores the United States' intervention in Haiti in the early 20th century. The intervention, which lasted from 1915 to 1934, aimed to stabilize the country amidst political turmoil and protect American interests, particularly in the sugar industry. The chapter examines the complex dynamics that led to the intervention, including economic concerns and perceived threats to American security.

Throughout the subchapter, readers will gain insights into the United States' strategic calculations, diplomatic maneuvering, and military actions during these interventions. It will shed light on the consequences of these interventions, both immediate and long-term, and their impact on the political, social, and economic landscapes of the Dominican Republic and Haiti.

By studying these cases, diplomats and individuals interested in American military interventions will gain a deeper understanding of the motivations, strategies, and outcomes of these interventions. The subchapter aims to provide a comprehensive analysis of the United States' "easy" wars and diplomatic maneuvering in the Caribbean, contributing to a broader understanding of American military interventions in small-scale conflicts and their implications on regional dynamics.

Analysis and Critiques of U.S. Involvement

In this subchapter, we delve into an in-depth analysis and critique of the United States' involvement in various conflicts and diplomatic maneuvers. By examining historical events and exploring the motivations behind U.S. military interventions, diplomats can gain a deeper understanding of American foreign policy and its implications for international relations.

One of the key aspects we explore is the United States' "Easy" Wars - the conflicts in Panama, Grenada, and Kuwait. These military interventions were characterized by swift and decisive action, but they also raised questions about the extent of American interventionism and its potential consequences. By critically evaluating these conflicts, diplomats can better comprehend the United States' approach to small-scale conflicts and its implications for regional stability.

Additionally, we examine the United States' military interventions in Latin America and the Caribbean, including Central America. These regions have witnessed significant American military involvement, often driven by perceived threats to American interests and the desire to maintain influence in the Western Hemisphere. By scrutinizing these interventions, diplomats can gain insights into the complexities of U.S.-Latin American relations and the long-term consequences of military actions in the region.

A crucial aspect of U.S. involvement discussed in this subchapter is the Panama Canal Zone and American military presence. The U.S. military's control over the Panama Canal, and subsequent interventions in Panama, have shaped the geopolitical landscape of the region. Understanding the historical context and implications of American military presence in the Panama Canal Zone is essential for diplomats working on issues related to the region.

Furthermore, we explore American military interventions during the Cold War and its impact on global dynamics. From covert operations in oil-rich countries to military engagements in small island nations, the United States sought to protect its interests and influence during this era. By critically analyzing these interventions, diplomats can assess the effectiveness and ethical implications of U.S. actions during the Cold War.

Ultimately, this subchapter provides diplomats with a comprehensive analysis and critique of U.S. involvement in various conflicts and diplomatic maneuvers. By understanding the motivations, consequences, and historical context of these interventions, diplomats can navigate the complexities of international relations and work towards fostering dialogue, cooperation, and peace.

U.S. Military Involvement in Central America

Central America has long been a region of interest for the United States, owing to its geographical proximity and perceived strategic importance. The U.S. military's involvement in Central America has been multifaceted, driven by a variety of factors such as Cold War politics, economic interests, and concerns over regional stability. This subchapter explores the historical context, motivations, and consequences of U.S. military interventions in this region.

During the Cold War era, Central America became a battleground for ideological struggles between the United States and the Soviet Union. The United States viewed the spread of communism in this region as a direct threat to its national security and, consequently, intervened militarily to counter perceived communist expansion. One notable example is the U.S. involvement in the civil wars of El Salvador and Nicaragua, where American forces provided military training, equipment, and financial aid to anti-communist forces.

Economic interests have also played a significant role in shaping U.S. military involvement in Central America. The region's rich natural resources, including agricultural products and minerals, have attracted American businesses. To protect these economic interests, the U.S. military has intervened in countries like Honduras and Guatemala, supporting friendly governments and suppressing popular uprisings that could potentially disrupt American access to vital resources.

The consequences of U.S. military involvement in Central America have been far-reaching and complex. While American interventions have sometimes achieved short-term objectives, such as preventing the rise of communist governments, they have also generated long-term consequences that have had adverse effects on regional stability. The United States' support for repressive regimes and counterinsurgency operations led to widespread human rights abuses, displacement, and political instability, which continue to haunt the region to this day.

For diplomats seeking a comprehensive understanding of U.S. military involvement in Central America, this subchapter provides valuable insights into the motivations and consequences of American interventions. By analyzing historical events and their impact on the region, diplomats can better comprehend the complexities of U.S. foreign policy and its implications for Central America's social, political, and economic landscape.

This subchapter also serves as a reminder of the importance of pursuing diplomatic solutions to conflicts and addressing the root causes of instability. By fostering dialogue, promoting democratic values, and supporting sustainable development, diplomats can contribute to building a more peaceful and prosperous Central America, free from the need for external military interventions.

Root Causes and Cold War Dynamics

In the subchapter "Root Causes and Cold War Dynamics," we delve into the underlying factors that shaped the United States' military interventions during the Cold War era. This chapter explores the intricate web of political, economic, and ideological dynamics that influenced American foreign policy decisions and military engagements in various regions.

The Cold War, a period of heightened tensions between the United States and the Soviet Union, played a significant role in shaping American military interventions. The ideological clash between capitalism and communism created a sense of urgency for the United States to safeguard its interests and contain the spread of communism globally. This led to the emergence of a doctrine known as the domino theory, which posited that if one country fell to communism, neighboring nations would also succumb to the same fate. Consequently, the United States felt compelled to intervene in conflicts to prevent the domino effect from occurring.

One of the key regions where Cold War dynamics influenced American military interventions was Latin America. Latin America became a battleground for ideological influence, as the United States sought to prevent the spread of communism in its backyard. American military interventions in countries like Panama, Grenada, and Kuwait were driven by perceived threats to American interests, whether it be protecting American citizens or safeguarding strategic resources.

Furthermore, the United States military involvement in Central America and the Caribbean was characterized by a combination of economic interests, political considerations, and the desire to maintain regional stability. The Panama Canal Zone and American military presence in the region were crucial in ensuring American control over a vital maritime route, guaranteeing access to resources and projecting American power.

American military interventions in oil-rich countries were driven by the need to protect access to vital energy resources. The Gulf region, with its vast oil reserves, became a focal point for American military operations. The perceived threat to American interests, whether it be from hostile regimes or regional instability, prompted military engagements aimed at maintaining control over these resources.

In conclusion, the subchapter "Root Causes and Cold War Dynamics" explores the complex interplay of political, economic, and ideological factors that influenced American military interventions during the Cold War era. The United States' desire to safeguard its interests, contain the spread of communism, and protect access to vital resources shaped its foreign policy decisions and military engagements in various regions. By understanding these root causes and the dynamics of the Cold War, diplomats can gain valuable insights into the historical context that underpins these interventions.

Nicaragua: The Contra War and U.S. Support

The subchapter "Nicaragua: The Contra War and U.S. Support" delves into the complex history of the Contra War and the significant role played by the United States in supporting the Contras. This chapter aims to provide diplomats with a comprehensive understanding of the United States' military intervention in Central America during the Cold War era.

The Contra War, also known as the Nicaraguan Revolution, took place from 1979 to 1990, following the overthrow of the Somoza dictatorship by the Sandinistas. The Sandinistas, led by Daniel Ortega, implemented socialist policies and received support from the Soviet Union and Cuba. This raised concerns in Washington about the spread of communism in the region and the potential threat to American interests.

In response, the United States covertly supported the Contras, a rebel group composed of former members of the Somoza regime, who aimed to overthrow the Sandinistas. The U.S. provided financial aid, weapons, and training to the Contras, despite an explicit congressional ban on such support.

The subchapter explores the reasons behind U.S. involvement in this conflict. It discusses the perceived threat to American interests, including the fear of a Soviet-aligned government in Central America, potential disruption of regional stability, and the protection of American investments in Nicaragua. It also examines the strategic importance of Nicaragua due to its proximity to the Panama Canal and its potential impact on American military presence in the region.

Furthermore, the chapter analyzes the consequences of U.S. support for the Contras. It discusses the ethical dilemma faced by American policymakers, as allegations of human rights abuses and atrocities committed by the Contras emerged. The chapter also explores the political and diplomatic repercussions of U.S. involvement in the conflict, including strained relations with other Latin American countries and international condemnation.

By delving into the complexities of the Contra War and U.S. support, this subchapter provides diplomats with a nuanced understanding of the United States' military intervention in Central America during the Cold War. It highlights the multifaceted motivations and consequences of this intervention, allowing diplomats to analyze similar situations in the future and make informed decisions based on historical context and lessons learned.

El Salvador and Guatemala: Counterinsurgency and Human Rights Concerns

Introduction:

The subchapter "El Salvador and Guatemala: Counterinsurgency and Human Rights Concerns" delves into the United States' military interventions in Central America during the Cold War era. This section examines the complexities of counterinsurgency efforts in El Salvador and Guatemala, shedding light on the human rights concerns that arose as a consequence. Addressing an audience of diplomats, this subchapter aims to provide a comprehensive understanding of the United States' involvement in these nations and its impact on the region.

Background on United States Military Interventions in Central America:

Throughout the Cold War, the United States regarded Central America as a critical battleground to combat communism and protect American interests. The subchapter explores the United States' military engagements in the region, particularly in El Salvador and Guatemala, highlighting the underlying motivations and strategic maneuvering.

Counterinsurgency Efforts and Human Rights Concerns:

The subchapter analyzes the United States' counterinsurgency efforts in El Salvador and Guatemala, focusing on the methods employed and the consequences faced by the local populations. It examines the role of American military advisors, training programs, and the provision of military aid to the respective governments. Furthermore, it delves into how these interventions led to egregious human rights violations, including extrajudicial killings, torture, and forced disappearances.

Impact on the Region:

By uncovering the human rights concerns that emerged from United States' military interventions, this subchapter outlines the lasting impact on the region. It addresses the repercussions on civilian populations, the erosion of trust in government institutions, and the exacerbation of social and political divisions. Additionally, it explores the long-term consequences of these interventions, including the perpetuation of cycles of violence and instability.

Reflections on Diplomatic Maneuvering:

Drawing on diplomatic perspectives, this subchapter examines the United States' diplomatic maneuvering during these interventions. It analyzes the rationale behind the decisions made by American diplomats and policymakers, assessing the ethical and strategic implications of their actions.

Conclusion:

In conclusion, the subchapter "El Salvador and Guatemala: Counterinsurgency and Human Rights Concerns" sheds light on the United States' military interventions in Central America during the Cold War era. By addressing human rights concerns, it highlights the ethical complexities of counterinsurgency efforts. This subchapter serves as a crucial resource for diplomats seeking to understand the historical context and consequences of American military interventions in Latin America, small-scale conflicts, and oil-rich countries. It encourages a comprehensive examination of these interventions to inform future diplomatic strategies and promote a more nuanced approach to foreign policy.

The Panama Canal Zone and American Military Presence

The Panama Canal Zone holds a significant place in the history of United States military interventions and diplomatic maneuvering. This subchapter delves into the complex relationship between the United States and Panama, shedding light on the motivations behind American military presence in the region.

The Panama Canal, considered an engineering marvel, became a crucial strategic asset for the United States in the early 20th century. With its completion in 1914, the canal facilitated maritime trade and provided a shortcut between the Atlantic and Pacific Oceans. However, the United States' interest in the canal went beyond its economic benefits.

The Panama Canal Zone was established as a U.S. territory, granting the American military exclusive control over the area. This presence served as a means of safeguarding American interests and projecting power in the region. The United States justified its military presence by highlighting the need for protecting the canal and ensuring its neutrality.

During the Cold War era, the Panama Canal Zone acquired even greater importance. It became a strategic outpost for the United States, allowing for surveillance and control over potential threats in the Caribbean and Latin America. The American military's involvement in the region was driven by concerns over communism and the spread of Soviet influence.

However, the American military presence in the Panama Canal Zone was not without controversy. The Panamanian people viewed it as a violation of their sovereignty and an imperialistic imposition. This led to growing tensions between the United States and Panama, culminating in the Panama Canal Treaty negotiations in the late 20th century.

The subchapter examines the diplomatic maneuvering undertaken by both countries during these negotiations. It explores the push and pull factors that eventually led to the transfer of the Panama Canal Zone's control to Panama in 1999. The United States had to navigate the delicate balance between protecting its interests and addressing Panamanian demands for sovereignty.

The Panama Canal Zone and American military presence exemplify the United States' pursuit of its perceived interests in the name of national security. The chapter sheds light on the complexities of American military interventions during the Cold War era and highlights the need for a nuanced understanding of U.S. foreign policy decisions.

This subchapter is a must-read for diplomats and individuals interested in understanding the historical context and motivations behind American military actions in the Panama Canal Zone. It offers valuable insights into the dynamics of U.S.-Panama relations and the consequences of American military interventions in small-scale conflicts.

Historical Background: Construction and Control of the Canal

The construction and control of the Panama Canal holds immense historical significance, shaping not only the geopolitical landscape but also the United States' approach to military interventions. This subchapter dives into the historical background of the canal, shedding light on the motivations behind its construction and the subsequent control exercised by the United States.

The idea of a canal connecting the Atlantic and Pacific Oceans dates back to the early 16th century when Spanish explorers first recognized the strategic advantage such a waterway would provide. It wasn't until the late 19th century that the concept gained significant traction, with the United States emerging as a key player in its realization.

After failed French attempts, the United States took over the construction of the canal in 1904, under the guidance of President Theodore Roosevelt. The primary motive behind this ambitious project was to establish a shorter and safer trade route between the Atlantic and Pacific, reducing the time and cost of transporting goods between the two coasts. Furthermore, the canal held immense strategic importance, allowing for quicker deployment of military assets in times of conflict.

The control of the canal, however, became a contentious issue. The Hay-Bunau-Varilla Treaty of 1903 granted the United States sovereignty over the Panama Canal Zone, a area stretching five miles on either side of the canal. This control was justified as a means to protect the canal's neutrality and ensure its secure operation. However, this arrangement sparked resentment among many Latin American nations, who saw it as a blatant display of American imperialism.

Throughout the Cold War, the United States fiercely guarded its control over the canal, viewing it as a vital asset in countering Soviet influence in the region. This period witnessed various military interventions in Latin America and the Caribbean, with the canal serving as a strategic hub for these operations.

The Panama Canal Zone and American military presence became synonymous, with the United States maintaining a significant military force in the area. However, growing tensions over sovereignty led to negotiations between the two countries, ultimately resulting in the 1977 Torrijos-Carter Treaties. These agreements marked a significant shift, gradually transferring control of the canal to Panama, which was finally completed on December 31, 1999.

The construction and control of the Panama Canal, as explored in this subchapter, provide a crucial historical context to understand the United States' military engagements in the region. From the initial motivations behind its construction to the subsequent control exercised by the United States, the canal played a central role in shaping American military interventions during the Cold War and beyond.

U.S. Military Operations in the Canal Zone

The United States' military operations in the Canal Zone have played a significant role in shaping American foreign policy and military strategy throughout history. The Canal Zone, situated in Panama, has been a critical strategic location, connecting the Atlantic and Pacific Oceans and serving as a vital trade route for global commerce. This subchapter will delve into the various military operations conducted by the United States in the Canal Zone, shedding light on their underlying motives and diplomatic implications.

The United States' military interventions in the Canal Zone can be traced back to the early 20th century when the construction of the

Panama Canal began. The U.S. military played a crucial role in ensuring the security and smooth operation of the canal. However, these military operations were not limited to safeguarding the canal's functionality; they also served as a means to exert American influence in the region.

During the Cold War era, the United States' military engagement in the Canal Zone intensified. The fear of communist expansion in Latin America prompted the deployment of American troops to protect American interests and prevent the spread of communism. This military presence in the Canal Zone allowed the U.S. to maintain control over the canal and safeguard its strategic advantages.

Furthermore, American military operations in the Canal Zone were not solely driven by political motives but also economic interests. The United States relied heavily on the uninterrupted flow of goods through the Panama Canal, particularly oil-rich countries in the Gulf region. As a result, the U.S. military interventions in the Canal Zone were often responses to perceived threats to American interests, such as potential disruptions to the oil supply.

This subchapter will also explore the smaller-scale conflicts in which the United States was involved in the Canal Zone. These conflicts ranged from military engagements in small island nations to interventions in Central America. The United States used these operations to flex its military muscle and establish dominance in the region, ensuring the protection of its economic and political interests.

In conclusion, the United States' military operations in the Canal Zone have been shaped by a complex interplay of factors, including geopolitics, economics, and diplomatic maneuvering. Understanding these military interventions is crucial for diplomats and individuals interested in comprehending the United States' historical involvement in the region and the broader implications for global politics.

Panama Canal Treaty and the End of American Presence

The Panama Canal Treaty of 1977 marked a significant turning point in the history of American presence in Panama and Latin America as a whole. This subchapter delves into the intricacies of this historic treaty and its implications for both the United States and Panama.

For decades, the United States had maintained a strong military and economic presence in the Panama Canal Zone, which allowed them to exercise considerable control over this vital waterway. However, growing anti-American sentiment in Panama, coupled with the global trend towards decolonization and self-determination, necessitated a reevaluation of the American presence in the region.

In an effort to address these concerns and pave the way for a more equal relationship between the two nations, negotiations began in the early 1970s for a new treaty that would ultimately lead to the transfer of the Panama Canal to Panamanian control. These negotiations were complex and fraught with challenges, as both sides sought to protect their own interests while also finding common ground.

The resulting Panama Canal Treaty, signed in 1977, set a timeline for the gradual transfer of control over the canal to Panama. It also stipulated that the United States would gradually reduce its military presence in the region, ultimately leading to the complete withdrawal of American forces by the year 2000.

This treaty was met with mixed reactions from various stakeholders. Diplomats and policymakers in the United States recognized the need for a more balanced and equitable relationship with Panama, and saw the treaty as a step in the right direction. They also understood that the American military presence in Panama had often been a source of tension and anti-American sentiment in the region.

However, some critics argued that the treaty represented a loss of American influence and control over a strategically important waterway. They expressed concerns about the potential impact on American national security and the ability to project military power in the region.

Nonetheless, the Panama Canal Treaty ultimately paved the way for the end of American presence in Panama and Latin America. It represented a shift towards a more cooperative and mutually beneficial relationship between the United States and Panama, and served as a model for future diplomatic engagements in the region.

The legacy of the Panama Canal Treaty is still felt today. It symbolizes the end of an era of American dominance in Latin America and the recognition of the importance of respecting the sovereignty and self-determination of nations in the region. It also serves as a reminder that diplomacy and negotiation can be powerful tools in resolving conflicts and fostering positive relationships between nations.

Chapter 3: U.S. Military Interventions During the Cold War

American Military Operations in the Gulf Region

The Gulf region has been a significant area of interest for the United States' military operations for several decades. The strategic importance of this region, which encompasses countries like Iraq, Iran, Saudi Arabia, and Kuwait, cannot be underestimated. This subchapter aims to provide a comprehensive understanding of American military operations in the Gulf region, exploring the motivations, strategies, and outcomes of these interventions.

From the early 20th century, the United States recognized the Gulf region's vital role in global geopolitics due to its abundant oil resources and its position as a crossroads between Europe, Asia, and Africa. This realization led to a series of military interventions and engagements that aimed to safeguard American interests, ensure stability, and protect access to oil reserves.

One of the most notable American military operations in the Gulf region was the Gulf War in 1990-1991. Following Iraq's invasion of Kuwait, the United States, along with a coalition of international partners, launched Operation Desert Storm to liberate Kuwait and restore stability in the region. This military campaign showcased the United States' military might and its commitment to safeguarding the interests of its allies.

Moreover, American military operations in the Gulf region have not been limited to large-scale conflicts like the Gulf War. The United States has also been involved in smaller-scale conflicts and military actions, such as targeted airstrikes, covert operations, and counterterrorism efforts. These operations aimed to respond to perceived threats to American interests, combat terrorism, and maintain regional stability.

It is important for diplomats to understand the underlying motivations behind American military operations in the Gulf region. While the protection of American interests, including access to oil, has been a driving factor, the United States has also sought to promote democracy, human rights, and regional stability. However, these operations have not been without controversy, often giving rise to debates about the extent of American intervention and its long-term consequences.

In conclusion, American military operations in the Gulf region have played a crucial role in shaping the geopolitical landscape of the region. From the Gulf War to counterterrorism efforts, the United States has demonstrated its commitment to protecting its interests and maintaining stability in this strategically important area. Diplomats must understand the complexities of these operations, the motivations behind them, and the potential ramifications for regional and global dynamics. Only through a comprehensive understanding can effective diplomatic maneuvering be achieved in the Gulf region.

The Iran-Iraq War and U.S. Involvement

The Iran-Iraq War, which lasted from 1980 to 1988, was a devastating conflict that had far-reaching implications for the Middle East and beyond. This subchapter will explore the role of the United States in this conflict, shedding light on the hidden agendas and diplomatic maneuvering that shaped American involvement.

The United States' interest in the Iran-Iraq War was primarily driven by its geopolitical considerations and its desire to protect its interests in the region. The war presented an opportunity for the U.S. to exert influence and maintain a balance of power in the Middle East. The United States had a complex relationship with both Iran and Iraq, and its involvement in the conflict was marked by a delicate balancing act.

Initially, the U.S. supported Iraq in its war against Iran, viewing Saddam Hussein's regime as a bulwark against the spread of Iranian influence in the region. The U.S. provided Iraq with financial aid, military intelligence, and even weapons, including chemical precursors. However, as the war progressed, it became clear that both sides were committing grave human rights abuses and using chemical weapons against each other. This put the U.S. in a difficult position, as it faced growing international criticism for its support of Iraq.

Moreover, the U.S. had its own agenda in the region, which included safeguarding its access to oil resources and countering the perceived threat of Iranian radicalism. The U.S. feared that Iran's Islamic revolution could inspire similar movements in other countries, jeopardizing American interests and regional stability. As such, the U.S. engaged in covert operations, such as providing military support to anti-Iranian groups and engaging in clandestine diplomacy.

The Iran-Contra scandal, which came to light in the late 1980s, exposed the extent of the U.S.'s involvement in the Iran-Iraq War. It was revealed that the U.S. had secretly sold weapons to Iran and used the proceeds to fund anti-Sandinista rebels in Nicaragua. This revelation further tarnished the U.S.'s reputation and raised questions about its moral standing in the international community.

In conclusion, the Iran-Iraq War and U.S. involvement in it were complex and multifaceted. The United States pursued its interests in the region, striving to maintain a balance of power and protect its access to oil resources. However, its actions were often driven by hidden agendas and diplomatic maneuvering, which ultimately had profound consequences for the people of Iran, Iraq, and the wider Middle East. Diplomats must be aware of these complexities and hidden motivations when analyzing American military interventions in small-scale conflicts.

Operation Desert Shield: Protecting Saudi Arabia

Chapter 4: Operation Desert Shield: Protecting Saudi Arabia

Introduction:

In the wake of Iraq's invasion of Kuwait in August 1990, the United States swiftly responded by launching Operation Desert Shield, a military operation aimed at protecting Saudi Arabia from potential aggression. This subchapter delves into the intricacies of this operation, highlighting the diplomatic maneuvering and the hidden agendas that underpinned the United States' involvement in the Gulf region.

Protecting Saudi Arabia:

Operation Desert Shield marked a crucial turning point in American military engagements in the Gulf region. Recognizing the strategic importance of Saudi Arabia as the world's leading oil producer, the United States swiftly deployed troops, ships, and aircraft to deter further Iraqi aggression and safeguard Saudi Arabia from any potential attacks. Diplomatic efforts were simultaneously initiated to garner international support, particularly from Arab nations, to form a collective defense against Iraq.

Diplomatic Maneuvering:

Behind the scenes, Operation Desert Shield was more than just a military operation. It was a carefully orchestrated diplomatic maneuver aimed at solidifying alliances and safeguarding American interests in the region. The United States engaged in intense negotiations with Saudi Arabia, offering assurances of military support in exchange for access to military bases and airfields. These negotiations were crucial in ensuring the smooth implementation of the operation and maintaining the delicate balance of power in the Gulf.

Hidden Agendas:

While the protection of Saudi Arabia was the stated objective of Operation Desert Shield, hidden agendas played a significant role in shaping the United States' actions. The preservation of global oil supplies and the containment of Saddam Hussein's regime were key factors driving American involvement. The fear of a potential domino effect, where other oil-rich countries in the region would be targeted, further motivated the United States to take swift and decisive action.

Implications and Legacy:

Operation Desert Shield ultimately served as a precursor to Operation Desert Storm, the military offensive that successfully liberated Kuwait from Iraqi occupation. The successful execution of both operations bolstered America's military prowess and cemented its role as a dominant force in the Gulf region. However, it also raised questions about American motives and the extent to which the United States was willing to intervene in small-scale conflicts to protect its own interests.

Conclusion:

Operation Desert Shield stands as a testament to the United States' ability to project power and protect its interests in the face of perceived threats. The diplomatic maneuvering and hidden agendas that shaped this operation provide valuable insights into the complexities of American military engagements in the Gulf region. As diplomats and individuals invested in understanding the United States' "easy" wars and military interventions, analyzing Operation Desert Shield sheds light on the delicate balance between diplomacy and military action in the pursuit of American interests.

Operation Desert Storm: Expelling Iraq from Kuwait

The subchapter "Operation Desert Storm: Expelling Iraq from Kuwait" delves into one of the most significant military interventions in recent history. Addressed to diplomats and the niches of various American military engagements, this subchapter aims to provide a comprehensive understanding of the events surrounding the expulsion of Iraq from Kuwait during the Gulf War.

The Gulf War, also known as the Persian Gulf War, was a result of Iraq's invasion of Kuwait in August 1990. Saddam Hussein, the then-president of Iraq, sought to annex Kuwait and control its vast oil reserves. This act of aggression threatened not only the stability of the Middle East but also the economic interests of numerous nations, especially the United States.

In response, the United States, under the leadership of President George H.W. Bush, formed an international coalition to expel Iraq from Kuwait. The operation began on January 17, 1991, with a massive aerial bombardment against Iraqi military targets. Over the next six weeks, the coalition forces, consisting of troops from various countries, engaged in ground operations to liberate Kuwait.

The subchapter analyzes the intricate diplomatic maneuvering that took place before and during the operation. It explores the United States' efforts to build a broad international coalition, garnering support from countries such as Saudi Arabia, Egypt, and Syria. The diplomats in the audience will gain insight into the diplomatic negotiations, the complex alliances formed, and the delicate balance of power in the region.

Moreover, the subchapter delves into the military strategies employed during Operation Desert Storm. It provides an overview of the air campaign, highlighting the use of advanced technology, such as precision-guided munitions and stealth aircraft. The ground offensive, which marked a turning point in the conflict, is also examined in detail, including the coalition's decisive victory against the Iraqi forces.

Furthermore, the subchapter sheds light on the geopolitical implications of the Gulf War. It discusses how the United States' intervention in Kuwait demonstrated its commitment to protecting its interests in the region, particularly oil resources. This analysis will resonate with those interested in American military interventions in oil-rich countries and actions taken in response to perceived threats to American interests.

In conclusion, "Operation Desert Storm: Expelling Iraq from Kuwait" provides diplomats and individuals interested in various American military engagements with a comprehensive account of the Gulf War. By exploring the diplomatic maneuvering, military strategies, and geopolitical implications, this subchapter offers valuable insights into the complexities of international relations and the United States' role in maintaining stability in the world.

U.S. Military Engagements in Small Island Nations

Small island nations have often found themselves at the center of U.S. military engagements, playing a significant role in shaping American foreign policy and military strategy. These island nations, often located strategically or rich in resources, have attracted the attention of the United States, leading to military interventions in various forms.

One such example of U.S. military involvement in small island nations is the case of Grenada. In 1983, the United States launched Operation Urgent Fury, a military intervention aimed at removing the Marxist government of Grenada. The U.S. justified its actions by citing concerns over the safety of American citizens and the potential threat posed by the construction of an airfield on the island. This military operation demonstrated the United States' willingness to intervene in small island nations to protect its strategic interests and assert its dominance in the region.

Similarly, the United States has been actively involved in the Caribbean, conducting military operations to safeguard its interests. For instance, during the Cold War, the United States intervened in the Dominican Republic in 1965 to prevent the spread of communism and protect American investments. This military engagement highlighted the United States' commitment to preserving its influence in the region and preventing the establishment of hostile governments.

The U.S. military has also played a significant role in Central America, particularly during the 1980s. American interventions in countries such as Nicaragua, El Salvador, and Panama aimed to counter perceived threats to American interests, including the spread of communism and the protection of the Panama Canal. These military engagements showcased the United States' willingness to employ military force to safeguard its strategic assets and prevent the rise of anti-American governments.

In addition to strategic considerations, the United States has also intervened in small island nations due to their valuable resources. Oil-rich countries, such as those in the Persian Gulf region, have been the focus of American military actions. The United States' military engagement in countries like Kuwait and Iraq has been driven by the need to protect its access to vital oil reserves, ensuring a stable and affordable energy supply.

In conclusion, U.S. military engagements in small island nations have been driven by a variety of factors, including strategic considerations, the protection of American interests, and the preservation of vital resources. These military interventions have shaped American foreign policy and diplomatic maneuvering, allowing the United States to exert its influence and maintain its dominance in various regions. As diplomats, understanding these historical military engagements is crucial in navigating international relations and formulating effective diplomatic strategies.

Intervention in Grenada Revisited

In this subchapter, we delve into the historical context and revisit the United States' military intervention in Grenada, shedding light on the hidden agendas and diplomatic maneuvering that shaped this controversial episode. Aimed at diplomats and individuals interested in American military actions, this subchapter provides a comprehensive analysis of the United States' "easy" war in Grenada, highlighting its significance in the broader framework of U.S. military interventions.

The intervention in Grenada took place in 1983 when the United States, under the Reagan administration, launched Operation Urgent Fury. The ostensible reason for this military action was to protect American citizens residing on the island and restore stability after a coup d'état. However, as we delve deeper, it becomes evident that there were ulterior motives behind this intervention.

One of the key factors behind the intervention was the fear of Grenada becoming a Soviet-Cuban outpost in the Caribbean. The Reagan administration believed that the construction of a new airport in Grenada, funded by Cuba, was a strategic move to facilitate Soviet military presence. This perceived threat to American interests in the region prompted the United States to take swift action.

However, as we analyze the events leading up to the intervention, it becomes apparent that the United States had long-standing interests in the Caribbean, particularly in countering leftist movements and securing its economic dominance. The fear of Grenada becoming a successful socialist experiment, similar to Cuba, further fueled the interventionist agenda.

Moreover, the United States' intervention in Grenada must also be viewed within the broader context of Cold War politics. With the Soviet Union's influence expanding in various parts of the world, the United States saw it as imperative to prevent any potential domino effect in the Caribbean. Grenada, with its socialist government and ties to Cuba, became a convenient target for American military action.

By revisiting the intervention in Grenada, this subchapter aims to shed light on the hidden agendas and diplomatic maneuvering that shaped the United States' military actions. It serves as a reminder that behind seemingly "easy" wars, there are complex geopolitical calculations and power dynamics at play. Understanding these nuances is crucial for diplomats and individuals interested in the intricacies of American military interventions in small-scale conflicts, the Caribbean, and oil-rich countries.

The Case of Haiti: Operations Uphold Democracy and Secure Tomorrow

Introduction:

In the annals of American military interventions, the case of Haiti stands as a complex and significant chapter. Operations Uphold Democracy and Secure Tomorrow shed light on the United States' efforts to stabilize the troubled nation, promote democracy, and safeguard American interests. This subchapter explores the intricacies of these operations, their historical context, and the diplomatic maneuvering behind them.

Historical Background:

Haiti's tumultuous past, marked by political instability, economic crises, and human rights abuses, necessitated international intervention. The United States had a vested interest in ensuring stability in the region, particularly in light of the Caribbean's strategic importance and America's historical ties to Haiti.

Operations Uphold Democracy and Secure Tomorrow:

Operations Uphold Democracy (1994-1995) and Secure Tomorrow (2004) were pivotal moments in Haiti's history. Uphold Democracy aimed to restore the democratically elected President Jean-Bertrand Aristide, who had been ousted in a military coup. Secure Tomorrow, on the other hand, focused on reestablishing stability after another political crisis erupted.

Diplomatic Maneuvering:

The United States, acting as a diplomatic mediator, played a key role in brokering agreements between conflicting Haitian factions. Diplomats skillfully navigated political minefields, working tirelessly to bring about peaceful resolutions and democratic transitions. These operations showcased the United States' commitment to upholding democratic values and promoting stability in the region.

Challenges and Successes:

The interventions in Haiti were not without challenges. They faced opposition from various factions within Haitian society and skepticism from the international community. However, these operations also achieved notable successes, such as the restoration of President Aristide and the establishment of a more stable political environment.

Legacy and Lessons Learned:

The case of Haiti serves as a valuable lesson in the complexities of military interventions. It highlights the delicate balance between promoting democracy, protecting American interests, and respecting the sovereignty of the host nation. The experiences in Haiti informed subsequent interventions and shaped US foreign policy in the region.

Conclusion:

Operations Uphold Democracy and Secure Tomorrow in Haiti demonstrated the United States' commitment to upholding democratic principles, promoting stability, and safeguarding its interests. The diplomatic maneuvering behind these operations showcased the depth of American engagement in the region and its willingness to act in response to perceived threats. The case of Haiti remains a significant chapter in the United States' military interventions, offering valuable insights to diplomats and scholars alike.

Lessons Learned and Controversies Surrounding Island Interventions

The United States' history of military interventions on small islands has been a subject of great interest and debate among diplomats and scholars. The subchapter "Lessons Learned and Controversies Surrounding Island Interventions" examines the experiences and consequences of American military actions in a range of island nations, with a particular focus on Panama, Grenada, and Kuwait. This subchapter aims to provide valuable insights and provoke critical thinking among diplomats who have a keen interest in understanding the dynamics of these "easy" wars and the diplomatic maneuvering that accompanied them.

One of the central lessons learned from these interventions is the importance of understanding the unique historical, political, and cultural contexts of the targeted island nations. In the case of Panama, the controversial military intervention in 1989 highlighted the complex relationship between the United States and the Panama Canal Zone. This intervention sparked significant debates regarding sovereignty, human rights, and the legitimacy of American military presence in the region. Similarly, the invasion of Grenada in 1983 raised concerns about the justification for intervention and the potential for unintended consequences.

Another critical aspect to consider is the long-term impact of these interventions on regional stability and the perception of the United

States. While some argue that American military actions in Latin America and the Caribbean were necessary to protect American interests and maintain stability, others criticize them as examples of "gunboat diplomacy" and imperialistic tendencies. These controversies have had lasting effects on diplomatic relations with affected nations, shaping the perception of American intervention in the region.

Furthermore, the subchapter delves into the role of the Cold War in shaping American military interventions on small islands. The strategic importance of these island nations in the context of the larger global ideological struggle was often a key factor in justifying military actions. The Gulf War in 1991, sparked by Iraq's invasion of Kuwait, showcased the United States' determination to protect its interests in the oil-rich region. This conflict highlighted the delicate balance between military intervention and diplomatic negotiations.

In conclusion, "Lessons Learned and Controversies Surrounding Island Interventions" serves as a comprehensive exploration of the United States' military engagements in small island nations, examining the historical, political, and cultural factors that shaped these interventions. It invites diplomats to critically analyze the lessons learned from these conflicts, the controversies they generated, and their long-term impact on American foreign policy. By understanding the intricacies of these interventions, diplomats can navigate future conflicts with more nuanced perspectives and effective diplomatic maneuvering.

American Military Interventions in Oil-Rich Countries

The United States has a long history of military interventions in oil-rich countries, driven by its strategic and economic interests. These interventions have often been disguised as efforts to uphold democracy, protect human rights, or ensure regional stability. However, a closer examination reveals hidden agendas and diplomatic maneuvering that serve the United States' own interests at the expense of other nations.

One of the key motivations behind American military interventions in oil-rich countries is to secure access to vital energy resources. The United States heavily relies on oil to fuel its economy and maintain its global influence. As a result, it has been willing to use military force to safeguard its access to oil reserves.

In the case of the Gulf region, the United States has repeatedly intervened militarily to protect its interests. The most notable example is the Gulf War in 1990-1991, when the United States led a coalition to liberate Kuwait from Iraqi occupation. While the official justification was to defend Kuwait's sovereignty, many argue that the real objective was to safeguard the region's oil supplies and prevent Saddam Hussein from gaining control over a significant portion of global oil reserves.

Similarly, American military interventions in Latin America and the Caribbean have often been driven by a desire to protect American economic interests, including oil. For instance, the United States has intervened in countries like Venezuela, Colombia, and Mexico, where it has sought to maintain favorable political and economic conditions for American oil companies.

These interventions have often had unintended consequences, such as exacerbating political instability, fueling anti-American sentiments, and undermining democratic processes. The United States' focus on securing oil resources has sometimes led to support for authoritarian regimes that guarantee stability and favorable conditions for American companies, but at the expense of human rights and democracy.

Diplomats must be aware of these hidden agendas and diplomatic maneuvering when dealing with American military interventions in oil-rich countries. They should critically examine the justifications put forth by the United States and consider the broader geopolitical and economic context. By understanding the underlying motives behind these interventions, diplomats can effectively navigate the complex dynamics and advocate for fair and equitable solutions that prioritize the interests of all nations involved.

In conclusion, American military interventions in oil-rich countries have been driven by the United States' strategic and economic interests, particularly its need for secure access to energy resources. Diplomats should be aware of the hidden agendas and diplomatic maneuvering that often accompany these interventions, and strive to promote fair and equitable solutions that prioritize the interests of all nations involved. Only by doing so can we foster genuine stability, democracy, and respect for human rights in these regions.

Iraq: From Kuwait to Operation Iraqi Freedom

In the subchapter titled "Iraq: From Kuwait to Operation Iraqi Freedom," we delve into the United States' involvement in Iraq, specifically focusing on the period spanning from the Gulf War to the controversial Operation Iraqi Freedom. This chapter aims to provide diplomats and those interested in American military interventions with an in-depth understanding of the intricate dynamics and hidden agendas that shaped these conflicts.

The story begins in 1990 when Iraq, under the leadership of Saddam Hussein, invaded Kuwait, triggering global outrage. The United States, concerned about protecting its interests in the region, swiftly assembled an international military coalition to liberate Kuwait. The Gulf War of 1991 marked the beginning of America's military engagements in Iraq.

However, as the years unfolded, it became apparent that American military involvement in Iraq had more profound implications. Hidden agendas and diplomatic maneuvering started to shape subsequent actions. The United States, wary of Saddam Hussein's regime and its potential threat to American interests, continued to assert its influence in the region.

Fast forward to 2003, and the world witnessed Operation Iraqi Freedom, a controversial military campaign launched by the United States with the aim of toppling Saddam Hussein's regime and eliminating weapons of mass destruction (WMDs). The decision to go to war was met with significant international opposition and sparked debates regarding the legitimacy of the invasion.

This subchapter examines the various factors that contributed to the United States' military interventions in Iraq. It explores the complex web of geopolitical interests, oil-rich resources, and perceived threats to American national security. It also sheds light on the diplomatic maneuvering that occurred behind the scenes, highlighting the delicate balance of power and the role of international alliances.

By delving into the historical context and analyzing the motivations behind these military actions, diplomats can gain a comprehensive understanding of the United States' involvement in Iraq. This knowledge becomes invaluable as diplomats navigate international relations, negotiate peace treaties, and seek to prevent future conflicts.

Ultimately, "Iraq: From Kuwait to Operation Iraqi Freedom" provides diplomats with crucial insights into the United States' "easy" wars and the diplomatic maneuvering that shaped them. It serves as a vital resource for understanding the complex dynamics of American military interventions, particularly in the Gulf region and oil-rich countries.

Libya: Operation Odyssey Dawn and Beyond

In the subchapter titled "Libya: Operation Odyssey Dawn and Beyond," we delve into the United States' military intervention in Libya and the subsequent diplomatic maneuvers that followed. This chapter is specifically addressed to diplomats and those interested in the United States' "easy" wars and diplomatic maneuvering. It also appeals to the niches of American military interventions in various regions such as

Latin America, the Caribbean, Central America, the Gulf region, small island nations, and oil-rich countries.

The United States' military involvement in Libya began with Operation Odyssey Dawn in 2011, in response to the escalating violence and human rights abuses perpetrated by the regime of Muammar Gaddafi. This military intervention was carried out under the auspices of a United Nations Security Council resolution, which authorized the establishment of a no-fly zone and the protection of civilians. The swift and decisive action taken by the United States, along with its international allies, marked a turning point in the Libyan conflict.

However, Operation Odyssey Dawn was just the beginning of a complex and multifaceted endeavor. Beyond the military intervention, the United States had to navigate the intricate web of diplomatic relations and engage in strategic maneuvering to ensure a stable and prosperous future for Libya. This involved working closely with international organizations, regional partners, and the Libyan Transitional National Council to facilitate the transition from a dictatorship to a democratic government.

The aftermath of Operation Odyssey Dawn presented unique challenges for the United States and its allies. The United States had to balance its desire to support the Libyan people in their quest for democracy with the need to safeguard its own interests and regional stability. This required careful diplomatic maneuvering to address the concerns of various stakeholders and mitigate potential conflicts.

Moreover, the United States' involvement in Libya had broader implications for its foreign policy in the region. It highlighted the delicate balance between humanitarian intervention and respect for sovereignty, as well as the challenges of nation-building in a post-conflict scenario. These lessons learned from Operation Odyssey Dawn would shape future American military interventions in small-scale conflicts and oil-rich countries, as well as its engagements in small island nations and responses to perceived threats to American interests.

In conclusion, the subchapter "Libya: Operation Odyssey Dawn and Beyond" explores the United States' military intervention in Libya and the subsequent diplomatic maneuvering that followed. It is a valuable resource for diplomats and those interested in the United States' "easy" wars and diplomatic strategies across various regions and conflicts.

Analyzing the Motivations and Outcomes of Oil-Rich Interventions

In the subchapter "Analyzing the Motivations and Outcomes of Oil-Rich Interventions," we delve into the complex relationship between the United States and oil-rich nations during various military interventions. This chapter aims to provide diplomats and specialists in the field with a comprehensive understanding of the motivations behind these interventions and the resulting outcomes.

Throughout history, the United States has been involved in a series of military actions in oil-rich countries, ranging from the Panama, Grenada, and Kuwait conflicts to interventions in Latin America, the Caribbean, Central America, and the Gulf region. These interventions were not solely driven by altruistic motives but rather influenced by a combination of geopolitical, economic, and strategic considerations.

One key motivation for these interventions was the protection of American interests. The United States, heavily reliant on oil imports, sought to secure access to these vital resources. Oil-rich countries became the center of attention due to their strategic importance and the potential threat that disruptions in oil supply could pose to the American economy and national security.

Another significant motivation was the desire to maintain stability in regions where American interests were at stake. The United States often intervened in situations where it perceived threats to its economic or political dominance. By intervening, the U.S. aimed to secure friendly governments, prevent the rise of anti-American sentiment, and maintain stability conducive to its economic and military presence.

However, the outcomes of these interventions were not always as intended. While some interventions achieved short-term objectives, they often led to unforeseen consequences in the long run. Instances of anti-American sentiment, increased regional tensions, or unintended consequences like the rise of extremist groups have occurred after interventions.

This subchapter also explores the impact of American military interventions on small island nations and their unique challenges. It delves into the historical context of the Panama Canal Zone and American military presence, highlighting the strategic importance of the region and the subsequent interventions.

Overall, "Analyzing the Motivations and Outcomes of Oil-Rich Interventions" provides diplomats and specialists with a comprehensive analysis of the United States' military actions in oil-rich countries and their underlying motivations. By examining both the intentions and outcomes of these interventions, this subchapter aims to facilitate a deeper understanding of the complexities involved and promote more informed decision-making in future diplomatic and military endeavors.

Chapter 4: U.S. Military Actions in Response to Perceived Threats to American Interests

Historical Background: The Monroe Doctrine and Beyond

The Monroe Doctrine, proclaimed by President James Monroe in 1823, marked a significant turning point in United States foreign policy. This doctrine outlined the nation's stance on European colonization in the Western Hemisphere and declared that any attempt by European powers to establish new colonies or interfere with the affairs of independent nations in the Americas would be viewed as a threat to the United States' interests.

The Monroe Doctrine was born out of a combination of factors. First, the United States had recently gained independence from Britain and was eager to assert itself as a sovereign nation. Second, there was a growing concern among American leaders about European powers reestablishing colonial control or influence in the Americas, which could potentially threaten American security and trade. Lastly, the doctrine reflected the broader sense of Manifest Destiny, the belief that the United States was destined to expand its territory and influence throughout North and South America.

In the decades that followed, the United States used the Monroe Doctrine as justification for various military interventions and diplomatic maneuverings in the Western Hemisphere. These interventions were often driven by a combination of economic interests, political ideology, and a desire to protect American citizens and assets abroad.

One notable example of American military intervention in the region was the Spanish-American War in 1898. The United States, motivated by a mixture of humanitarian concerns and a desire for strategic control in the Caribbean, intervened in the Cuban struggle for independence from Spain. This conflict resulted in the United States gaining control over territories such as Puerto Rico and the Philippines, further solidifying its influence in the region.

Throughout the 20th century, the United States continued to assert its dominance in the Western Hemisphere through military actions and diplomatic maneuvering. From military interventions in Latin America and the Caribbean to its involvement in Central America and small island nations, the United States consistently pursued its interests and sought to protect its strategic assets, such as the Panama Canal Zone.

The historical background of the Monroe Doctrine and its subsequent impact on American foreign policy is crucial for diplomats to understand. It provides a foundation for comprehending the motivations and justifications behind the United States' "easy" wars and diplomatic maneuvering in the regions mentioned above. By delving into this history, diplomats can gain a deeper insight into the complex dynamics that have shaped the United States' military engagements and interventions throughout history.

The Evolution of American Foreign Policy in the Western Hemisphere

Introduction:

In the subchapter titled "The Evolution of American Foreign Policy in the Western Hemisphere," we delve into the intricate web of diplomatic maneuvering, military interventions, and hidden agendas that have shaped the United States' approach to the Western Hemisphere. This chapter aims to provide diplomats, particularly those concerned with the United States' "Easy" Wars, military interventions, and engagements in various regions, with a comprehensive understanding of the historical context and evolution of American foreign policy in the Western Hemisphere.

Historical Context:

The United States' engagement in the Western Hemisphere has a rich and complex history. From the Monroe Doctrine of 1823 to the present day, American foreign policy has been guided by a desire to protect its interests and maintain influence in the region. The doctrine proclaimed American hegemony over the Western Hemisphere, warning European powers against any new colonial ventures. This policy set the stage for future interventions and military actions.

Cold War Era:

During the Cold War, the United States perceived threats to its interests in Latin America and the Caribbean. This led to numerous military interventions, covert operations, and support for authoritarian regimes. The United States military involvement in Latin America aimed to prevent the spread of communism and protect American interests in the region.

Small Island Nations and Oil-Rich Countries:

In addition to Latin America and the Caribbean, the United States has also been engaged in small island nations and oil-rich countries. American military engagements in small island nations, like Grenada, aimed to maintain stability and protect American citizens. Similarly, military interventions in oil-rich countries were driven by the desire to secure vital energy resources and safeguard American economic interests.

The "Easy" Wars:

The United States' military actions in Panama, Grenada, and Kuwait, often referred to as the "Easy" Wars, were characterized by relatively swift victories. These interventions showcased the United States' military prowess and demonstrated its commitment to protecting its interests and allies in the region.

Conclusion:

The evolution of American foreign policy in the Western Hemisphere has been shaped by a complex interplay of diplomatic maneuvering, military interventions, and perceived threats to American interests. From the Monroe Doctrine to the present day, the United States has sought to maintain its influence in the region, protect its economic interests, and respond to perceived threats. By understanding this historical context, diplomats can navigate the intricacies of American foreign policy in the Western Hemisphere and forge productive relationships with the United States.

The Roosevelt Corollary and the Doctrine's Influence

In the annals of American diplomacy, few policies have had a more profound and lasting impact than the Roosevelt Corollary. First articulated by President Theodore Roosevelt in 1904, this doctrine marked a significant departure from traditional American foreign policy and set the stage for the United States' future military interventions around the world.

At its core, the Roosevelt Corollary was an extension of the Monroe Doctrine, which had been declared nearly a century earlier. While the Monroe Doctrine sought to prevent European colonization in the Western Hemisphere, the Roosevelt Corollary went a step further by asserting the United States' right to intervene militarily in the affairs of Latin American nations to maintain stability and protect American interests.

The rationale behind the Corollary was twofold. First, it was seen as a response to the growing influence of European powers in the region, particularly in the aftermath of the Spanish-American War. By asserting its own dominance, the United States aimed to prevent any potential encroachments on its sphere of influence.

Second, the Corollary reflected a broader belief in the United States' duty to promote democracy and economic development in the Western Hemisphere. This vision of American exceptionalism justified military interventions as a means to spread democratic values and protect American investments in countries seen as unstable or under threat.

The influence of the Roosevelt Corollary was felt most acutely in the United States' "easy" wars in Panama, Grenada, and Kuwait. In each of these conflicts, the doctrine provided a legal and moral justification for American military action. Whether it was the removal of Manuel Noriega in Panama, the ousting of the Marxist government in Grenada, or the liberation of Kuwait from Iraqi forces, the Roosevelt Corollary provided the framework for intervention.

Beyond these specific conflicts, the doctrine's influence extended to American military interventions in Latin America, the Caribbean, and small island nations. From the Banana Wars in Central America to the military presence in the Panama Canal Zone, the United States' military actions during the Cold War were driven, in part, by the belief that it had a responsibility to protect its interests and promote stability in the region.

Furthermore, the doctrine's influence can be seen in American military engagements in oil-rich countries and small-scale conflicts. In response to perceived threats to American interests, such as the nationalization of oil resources or the rise of communist insurgencies, the United States invoked the Roosevelt Corollary to justify its military interventions.

In conclusion, the Roosevelt Corollary and its subsequent influence on American foreign policy cannot be overstated. By asserting the right to intervene militarily in Latin America and beyond, the United States set a precedent for future military interventions and shaped the course of diplomacy for decades to come. As diplomats, it is vital to understand the historical context and implications of the doctrine to navigate the complexities of international relations in the present day.

American Military Interventions in Small-Scale Conflicts

Introduction:

In this subchapter, we will delve into the American military interventions in small-scale conflicts, focusing on the United States' "easy" wars and diplomatic maneuvering. This chapter aims to provide diplomats with a comprehensive understanding of the United States' military actions in various regions, including Latin America, the Caribbean, Central America, Gulf region, small island nations, and oil-rich countries.

1. The United States' "Easy" Wars: Panama, Grenada, and Kuwait:

The United States has been involved in several "easy" wars throughout history, characterized by swift military operations and limited casualties. This section will explore the motives behind these interventions, the diplomatic strategies employed, and the long-term consequences of these actions.

2. United States Military Interventions in Latin America:

Latin America has been a significant region of interest for the United States, with numerous military interventions over the years. This section will discuss the reasons behind these interventions, including the perceived threats to American interests, diplomatic maneuvering, and the impact on the region's political and social landscape.

3. American Military Actions in the Caribbean:

The United States has a long history of military involvement in the Caribbean, often driven by concerns over regional stability, drug trafficking, and protection of American interests. This section will examine the motives behind these interventions, the diplomatic efforts undertaken, and the consequences for the affected countries.

4. U.S. Military Involvement in Central America:

Central America has witnessed significant American military involvement, particularly during the Cold War era. This section will analyze the reasons behind these interventions, including the containment of communism, diplomatic maneuvering, and the long-term effects on the region's political and economic development.

5. The Panama Canal Zone and American Military Presence:

The Panama Canal Zone holds strategic importance for the United States, leading to its military presence in the region. This section will explore the history of American military involvement in the Canal Zone, the diplomatic negotiations surrounding its presence, and the eventual transfer of control to Panama.

6. U.S. Military Interventions during the Cold War:

The Cold War era witnessed numerous American military interventions worldwide, driven by the perceived threat of communism. This section will examine the diplomatic strategies employed, the rationale behind these interventions, and the impact on global politics.

7. American Military Operations in the Gulf Region:

The Gulf region has been a focal point of American military interventions due to its rich oil reserves and geopolitical significance. This section will discuss the motives behind these interventions, diplomatic maneuvering, and the long-term consequences for the region.

8. U.S. Military Engagements in Small Island Nations:

Small island nations have not been immune to American military interventions, often driven by concerns over regional stability and protection of American interests. This section will explore the reasons behind these interventions, diplomatic efforts undertaken, and the impact on these nations' sovereignty.

9. American Military Interventions in Oil-Rich Countries:

The United States' military interventions in oil-rich countries have been driven by the need to protect its energy security and strategic interests. This section will analyze the diplomatic strategies employed, the motives behind these interventions, and the impact on global energy dynamics.

10. U.S. Military Actions in Response to Perceived Threats to American Interests:

Throughout history, the United States has responded to perceived threats to its interests through military interventions. This section will examine the diplomatic maneuvering, the motives behind these actions, and the consequences for American foreign policy.

Conclusion:

This subchapter provides diplomats with an in-depth analysis of American military interventions in small-scale conflicts, shedding light on the motives, diplomatic strategies, and long-term consequences of these actions. By understanding the historical context and lessons learned, diplomats can navigate future international crises with greater insight and effectiveness.

The Philippines: Spanish-American War and Insurgency

The Philippines holds a significant place in the history of the United States' "easy" wars and diplomatic maneuvering. The Spanish-American

War, which began in 1898, marked a turning point for both countries and set the stage for subsequent American military interventions in the region.

The war between Spain and the United States was initially fought over Cuba's struggle for independence. However, it quickly expanded to include the Philippines, which had been a Spanish colony for over 300 years. The United States saw an opportunity to extend its influence in the Pacific and gain access to valuable trade routes and resources.

In a swift and decisive victory, American forces defeated the Spanish fleet in the Battle of Manila Bay. With the capture of Manila, the United States effectively took control of the Philippines. However, this victory was just the beginning of a long and complex relationship between the two nations.

The Philippine people, who had been fighting for their independence from Spain, were not content with their new colonial masters. Led by figures such as Emilio Aguinaldo, they launched a guerrilla insurgency against the American occupation. The United States responded with a brutal counterinsurgency campaign, employing tactics such as forced relocation and scorched-earth policies.

This protracted conflict, known as the Philippine-American War, lasted until 1902 and resulted in the deaths of tens of thousands of Filipinos. The United States eventually quelled the insurgency and established a colonial government in the Philippines. However, the war had a lasting impact on the country's political and social landscape.

The United States' involvement in the Philippines during the Spanish-American War and the subsequent insurgency reflected its desire to expand its influence in the Pacific and protect its economic and strategic interests. It also demonstrated the willingness of the United States to use military force to assert its dominance in the region.

For diplomats and those interested in American military interventions, the Philippines' history provides valuable insights into the complexities of foreign policy and the challenges of maintaining control over a restless population. The lessons learned from this chapter in history continue to shape American military engagements in small-scale conflicts, interventions in oil-rich countries, and responses to perceived threats to American interests. Understanding the Spanish-American War and the Philippine-American War is crucial for comprehending the United States' role in the world and its approach to international conflicts.

Cuba: Bay of Pigs Invasion and the Cuban Missile Crisis

Throughout history, the United States has been involved in various military interventions and diplomatic maneuverings across the globe. One significant chapter in this narrative is the story of Cuba, which includes the infamous Bay of Pigs invasion and the Cuban Missile Crisis. These events not only shaped the course of American military interventions during the Cold War but also had lasting implications on the geopolitical landscape of the Caribbean and Latin America.

The Bay of Pigs invasion, which took place in April 1961, was a covert operation carried out by the Central Intelligence Agency (CIA) with the objective of overthrowing the Cuban government led by Fidel Castro. The plan involved training and arming a group of Cuban exiles to invade the island and spark a popular uprising against Castro's regime. However, the invasion was a colossal failure, with the Cuban military quickly suppressing the rebels and capturing many of them. This embarrassing defeat not only damaged the credibility of the United States but also strengthened Castro's grip on power, leading to a further deterioration of U.S.-Cuba relations.

Following the Bay of Pigs invasion, the Cuban Missile Crisis unfolded in October 1962, marking one of the most perilous moments of the Cold War. The crisis began when the United States discovered that the

Soviet Union was secretly installing nuclear missiles in Cuba, capable of reaching major U.S. cities. This revelation sparked a tense standoff, with the world on the brink of a nuclear war. Diplomatic negotiations and intense military posturing ensued, as the United States demanded the removal of the missiles, while the Soviet Union sought assurances for the security of Cuba. Eventually, a compromise was reached, with both superpowers agreeing to deescalate the situation by removing missiles from Cuba and Turkey, respectively.

These two events, the Bay of Pigs invasion and the Cuban Missile Crisis, highlighted the United States' military actions in response to perceived threats to American interests. They also underscored the delicate balance of power during the Cold War, as well as the importance of diplomatic maneuvering in averting catastrophic confrontations. Moreover, these episodes demonstrated the lasting impact of U.S. military interventions in small-scale conflicts and the complexities of American military involvement in Latin America and the Caribbean.

For diplomats and those interested in the United States' "easy" wars and diplomatic maneuvering, understanding the lessons and consequences of the Bay of Pigs invasion and the Cuban Missile Crisis is crucial. These events serve as cautionary tales, reminding us of the importance of informed decision-making, effective diplomacy, and the careful consideration of long-term consequences in future military interventions and diplomatic engagements.

Assessing the Legitimacy and Effectiveness of U.S. Responses

In "Hidden Agendas: The United States' 'Easy' Wars and Diplomatic Maneuvering," we delve into the complex web of the United States' military interventions and actions across various regions and conflicts. As diplomats, it is crucial to critically examine the legitimacy and effectiveness of these responses to truly understand the impact they had on global politics and relations.

The United States' "Easy" Wars: Panama, Grenada, and Kuwait, showcased the nation's willingness to use military force to protect its interests. However, questions arise regarding the legitimacy of these interventions. Were they truly necessary or a display of power? Did the United States exhaust diplomatic avenues before resorting to military action? As diplomats, we must assess the justifications and weigh the long-term consequences of such interventions.

Similarly, United States military interventions in Latin America and American military actions in the Caribbean have left lasting impacts on the region. Were these interventions driven by genuine concerns for democracy and stability, or were they motivated by economic and political interests? Assessing the legitimacy of these actions is vital to understanding the United States' role in shaping the region's geopolitical landscape.

Moreover, the United States' military involvement in Central America and the Panama Canal Zone and American military presence raise questions about the effectiveness of these interventions. Did they achieve their intended objectives, or did they exacerbate existing conflicts? Evaluating the outcomes and the long-term effects on regional stability is essential for diplomats seeking to foster positive relations with these nations.

Examining U.S. military interventions during the Cold War and American military operations in the Gulf region allows us to understand the rationale behind these actions. Were they driven by a genuine desire to protect American interests and contain communism, or were they influenced by ulterior motives? As diplomats, we must assess the legitimacy of these responses to gauge their impact on international relations.

Furthermore, American military engagements in small island nations, military interventions in oil-rich countries, and actions in response to perceived threats to American interests require a critical evaluation of the United States' role as a global superpower. Did these interventions effectively safeguard American interests, or did they undermine diplomatic efforts? Analyzing the legitimacy and effectiveness of these responses is essential for diplomats navigating the complexities of global politics.

In conclusion, "Hidden Agendas: The United States' 'Easy' Wars and Diplomatic Maneuvering" provides a comprehensive exploration of the United States' military interventions across various regions and conflicts. As diplomats, it is our responsibility to critically assess the legitimacy and effectiveness of these responses to foster positive relations and promote peace in the international arena.

Conclusion: Diplomatic Maneuvering and Hidden Agendas

Examining the recurring patterns and underlying motivations

In the subchapter "Examining the Recurring Patterns and Underlying Motivations" of the book "Hidden Agendas: The United States' 'Easy' Wars and Diplomatic Maneuvering," we delve into the intricate web of events that have shaped the United States' military interventions and diplomatic maneuvering over the years. This subchapter aims to provide diplomats with a deeper understanding of the recurring patterns and underlying motivations behind these actions.

The United States' "Easy" Wars, including Panama, Grenada, and Kuwait, have often been characterized by swift military interventions aimed at achieving specific objectives. These conflicts share common elements, such as a perception of threats to American interests, the presence of natural resources, and the strategic location of the nations involved. By examining these patterns, diplomats can gain valuable insights into the decision-making processes that have guided U.S. military interventions.

Furthermore, this subchapter explores the United States' military interventions in Latin America, the Caribbean, and Central America. These regions have been the stage for numerous American military actions, driven by a combination of strategic, economic, and political considerations. By examining the underlying motivations, diplomats can better understand the historical context and the long-lasting impact of these interventions on regional dynamics.

Another significant aspect covered in this subchapter is the United States' military involvement in small island nations. These nations, often characterized by their vulnerability and limited resources, have been subject to American military engagements for various reasons, including the protection of American interests, the prevention of ideological influences, or the safeguarding of strategic military bases. Diplomats can gain valuable insights into the dynamics of these interventions through a comprehensive examination of the recurring patterns and motivations.

Lastly, this subchapter delves into American military interventions in oil-rich countries and small-scale conflicts. The pursuit of energy resources and the desire to maintain stability in regions with potential security threats have been recurring motivations behind these interventions. By examining these patterns, diplomats can uncover the hidden agendas behind these actions and better navigate complex diplomatic environments.

In conclusion, the subchapter "Examining the Recurring Patterns and Underlying Motivations" provides diplomats with a comprehensive analysis of the United States' military interventions across various regions and conflicts. By understanding the recurring patterns and underlying motivations, diplomats can enhance their diplomatic maneuvering and engage in more informed decision-making processes. This knowledge is crucial for diplomats seeking to foster peaceful resolutions, protect national interests, and maintain stability in an ever-changing global landscape.

Analyzing the impact on diplomatic relations and global perceptions

In the complex realm of international relations, understanding the impact of military interventions and their implications on diplomatic relations and global perceptions is paramount. This subchapter aims to shed light on the intricate dynamics that unfold when the United States engages in what are often labeled as "easy" wars. By delving into the cases of Panama, Grenada, and Kuwait, as well as broader themes such as U.S. military interventions in Latin America, the Caribbean, Central America, and oil-rich countries, we will explore how these actions have shaped diplomatic relations and influenced global perceptions of the United States.

The United States' military interventions have undeniably left a lasting mark on diplomatic relations. Whether it was the invasion of Panama in 1989 to remove General Manuel Noriega, the swift operation in Grenada in 1983, or the liberation of Kuwait in 1991, these actions have prompted both praise and criticism from the international community. Diplomatic relations with countries involved, such as Panama, Grenada, and Kuwait, were inevitably impacted, with varying degrees of long-term consequences. By examining the aftermath of these interventions, diplomats can gain valuable insights into the intricacies of rebuilding diplomatic ties and managing the expectations of affected nations.

Furthermore, analyzing the broader context of U.S. military interventions in Latin America, the Caribbean, and Central America reveals a pattern of perceived American dominance. The Panama Canal Zone and American military presence in the region have often been viewed as asserting U.S. hegemony, leading to strained relations with neighboring countries. Similarly, U.S. military interventions during the Cold War, fueled by the fear of communism, have created enduring perceptions of American interventionism and undermined trust in the region.

Additionally, American military operations in the Gulf region and interventions in oil-rich countries have significantly shaped global perceptions. The notion of the United States intervening in these regions to safeguard its interests and access to resources has sparked debates on neo-colonialism and the pursuit of economic superiority. Diplomats must navigate these perceptions and work towards building mutual understanding and trust to ensure stable diplomatic relations.

Lastly, the United States' military engagements in small island nations and interventions in small-scale conflicts have often gone unnoticed on the global stage. However, these actions should not be overlooked, as they can still have a profound impact on diplomatic relations and shape global perceptions of U.S. foreign policy. Understanding the motivations and consequences of these interventions is crucial for diplomats to respond effectively to similar situations in the future.

In conclusion, analyzing the impact of U.S. military interventions on diplomatic relations and global perceptions is crucial for diplomats navigating the complexities of international relations. By examining specific cases and broader themes, diplomats can gain valuable insights into the intricacies of rebuilding diplomatic ties, managing perceptions, and fostering mutual understanding. Ultimately, this knowledge can contribute to more effective and nuanced diplomatic strategies in the face of future challenges.

Reflections on the future of U.S. military interventions and diplomacy

The future of U.S. military interventions and diplomacy is a topic of great importance, especially for diplomats who are involved in shaping the nation's foreign policy. In this subchapter, we will critically analyze the United States' "easy" wars and diplomatic maneuvering, shedding light on the hidden agendas behind these interventions.

The United States' "Easy" Wars: Panama, Grenada, and Kuwait

The United States' military interventions in Panama, Grenada, and Kuwait were deemed as "easy" wars due to their swift and decisive outcomes. However, it is crucial to reflect on the implications of such interventions. We must ask ourselves if these interventions were driven by genuine concerns for democracy and human rights, or if they were merely strategic maneuvers to protect American interests.

United States Military Interventions in Latin America

Latin America has been a region where the United States has frequently intervened militarily. As diplomats, we need to examine the long-term effects of these interventions and assess whether they have truly contributed to regional stability and development, or if they have perpetuated a cycle of dependence and instability.

American Military Actions in the Caribbean

The United States has a history of military actions in the Caribbean, often in response to perceived threats to American interests. It is vital for diplomats to evaluate the effectiveness of these interventions and consider alternative approaches, such as diplomacy and economic cooperation, to address challenges in the region.

U.S. Military Involvement in Central America

Central America has witnessed significant U.S. military involvement, especially during the Cold War era. As diplomats, we must reflect on the consequences of these interventions, including their impact on regional politics, social stability, and economic development. It is essential to learn from past experiences and explore more sustainable and diplomatic solutions to address issues in the region.

The Panama Canal Zone and American Military Presence

The United States' military presence in the Panama Canal Zone has long been a contentious issue. Diplomats should analyze the historical context of this presence and evaluate its impact on U.S.-Panama relations and regional dynamics. This reflection will help us navigate future diplomatic challenges and promote mutually beneficial partnerships.

In conclusion, this subchapter provides diplomats with an opportunity to reflect on the future of U.S. military interventions and diplomacy. By critically examining the hidden agendas behind the United States' "easy" wars and diplomatic maneuvering, diplomats can play a crucial role in shaping a more effective and ethical foreign policy. It is through introspection and open dialogue that we can ensure a more peaceful and prosperous future for both the United States and the nations affected by these interventions.